Mr. Stevens' Secretary

2017 finalist
MILLER WILLIAMS
poetry prize

Mr. Stevens' Secretary

poems by

Frances Schenkkan

The University of Arkansas Press
Fayetteville
2017

21 20 19 18 17   5 4 3 2 1

Designed by Liz Lester

⊗ The paper used in this publication meets the minimum
requirements of the American National Standard for
Permanence of Paper for Printed Library Materials Z39.48-1984.

Library of Congress Control Number: 2016956686

For Pete, who believed

SERIES EDITOR'S PREFACE

Miller Williams was the first editor to spot me, you might say, and subsequently, the one who published my first full-length book of poems, *The Apple That Astonished Paris*, in 1988. With a single stroke, I was transformed into a "published poet," an all-too-common phrase that reminds us of the vast number of poets who are unpublished, or as an optimist might say, "pre-published." Funny, we don't hear much about "unpublished novelists" or "unpublished journalists."

Since then, I have felt a special debt to Miller for the validation he gave me and for the delicacy with which he edited that collection. "You have a line that goes, 'I can see it so clearly.' I don't think you need that intensifier '*so*,'" he told me in our first talk on the phone. I was left with the feeling that this man had read my poems more closely and carefully than I had. I won't forget that initial phone call. Miller happened to find me in a hotel in Miami, where I was getting dressed to go to Hialeah for a day at the races. When I heard him say he was going to publish my book, I knew I'd been granted more than enough luck for one day; it was a pleasure to spend the afternoon losing one race after another. I wasn't just someone who couldn't pick a winner; I was a *published poet* who couldn't pick a winner. The day was made even better because my best pal was with me, and we even ran into Carol Flake, whose horse book, *Tarnished Crown*, was just about to be published.

Judging this prize, which is named in honor of the cofounder and director of the University of Arkansas Press, gives me the opportunity to pass on the gift that Miller Williams gave to me, the publication of a book of poems, in some cases a first book. For a poet, in terms of sheer thrills, there is no publication that matches his or her first book. With all this in mind, it follows that serving as judge for the Miller Williams Poetry Prize is great pleasure for me.

Even if one is so blissfully egalitarian and nonjudgmental as to believe that all poetry manuscripts are equal, one must concede that some are more equal than others. This year, all of the "more equal" ones were eye-openers for me, literary wake-up calls that brought me to attention, each for a very different reason.

Self-Portrait in a Door-Length Mirror might be an intentional echo of Ashbery's convex mirror, but Stephen Gibson's language is neither coy nor elliptical as Ashbery's typically is. Instead, Gibson presents a series of clear formalist poems, each organized around a different kind of patterning. A series of 8 seven-line poems—each in the rectangular shape of a painting—examines the life and art of Pierre Bonnard. But the focus is Marthe de Méligny, Bonnard's lover, model, and eventually, his wife. The eroticism of Marthe washing her feet in a bathtub or being submerged in it naked is balanced by the mention of the objects in the painting where "everything alive . . . is dead." Add to this grouping an intricately successful pantoum about Diane Arbus, along with my favorite, a twenty-seven-line monorhyme (a tour de force, by the way) written in reaction to a photograph of Hermann Göring's suicide. The radical subjects of Arbus (also a suicide) and SS Commander Göring are brought under control by the imposition of form. The resulting tension shows this exceptional poet at his rhyming best.

Mr. Stevens' Secretary—yes, it's *that* Mr. Stevens—is a series of vignettes taken from (or invented to create) the life of the great modernist's secretary. We see what Stevens looked like from her point of view, which includes how Stevens smelled—not bad as it turns out: "Oriental . . . but that may be that was because of the tea . . . white peony tea." A mild eroticism builds when we are told that the secretary keeps a special bottle of Chantilly "not at home but in her desk." We also get to see the secretary outside of her job in a poem about wasps and marriage and another about her pre-Stevens employers. But it is the famous poet who cannot distinguish *its* from *it's*. In another poem, she attempts to write a fable in which a father saves a cat who got its head stuck in a milk bottle, yet he has an awful temper and shouts "horribly" at his wife. Like Carol Ann Duffy's boldly feminist collection, *The World's Wife*, Frances Schenkkan's *Mr. Stevens' Secretary* forces readers to adjust their perspective by showing a great man through the eyes of a previously silent and less visible woman.

One requirement for poets is the ability to write about two different things at the same time. Seamus Heaney turns writing into a kind of digging. John Ciardi intertwines marriage and the structure of an arch. Among the several poems in Jennifer Givhan's *Protection Spell* that stopped me cold is "The Polar Bear," in which a mother tries to protect her black child from the television news of racial unrest (riots, arrests, brutality) by turning his attention to the Discovery Channel. But there, a polar bear is fighting for survival surrounded by vicious walruses and melting ice. The boy clutches his stuffed white bear and asks if this is real. Life in the Arctic and life in the urban streets are conjoined, ecology and racism wed. Givhan is a poet of great heart and brave directness who writes real-life poems, sometimes crowded to the point of claustrophobia with the details of life in the poor lane. One poem transforms a laundromat woman living "paycheck to paycheck" into a "god." Another poem is a stirring defense of cheerleaders, written without a drop of irony. A reader will be quick to trust the authority in this poet's voice and the credentials of experience that are on full display.

Not all the poems in *The Wild Night Dress* by Laura McCullough use scientific or technological language, but many of them do, and in ways that create interesting effects. This poet has the kind of binocular vision that can see the poetic and scientific aspects of the world simultaneously. The poem "Feed" opens: "In a drone video of Humpbacks / feeding off the coast of Canada, / the surface of the ocean is frothed into blossoms." The ending of that last line returns the poem to poetry's musical origins without implying any friction between this lovely sound and drone technology. In a poem in which the speaker hungers for eggs, this mix of diction occurs: "though I wish to fill myself, / until the ventromedial hypothalamus [the gland that stimulates hunger] / is so stimulated / all I can think of is flowers." This shuffling together of lyrical/ botanical and medical language is done so gracefully, it has the effect of bringing "the two cultures" into a rare state of peaceful coexistence. Also engaging are the more traditionally lyric poems, one about childhood, another about a "fawn caught in the family compost" (for me, an echo of the cat caught in a milk bottle in *Mr. Stevens' Secretary*), but the distinction this collection can best claim is the way the poems find an easy synthesis between poetry and science. Perhaps Laura McCullough's most telling confession lies in this couplet: "I can't help loving / the word *sonoluminescence*."

I'm glad that early on, the editors at the press and I agreed that the judge for these prizes should not be looking for poems that sound like the poems of Miller Williams but for poems that Miller might have enjoyed and admired. It's easy for me to picture Miller paging through these four books with a look of appreciation and even delight on his face, though he might keep a red pencil nearby just in case he comes across one of those annoying, unnecessary "intensifiers."

Billy Collins

ACKNOWLEDGMENTS

Some of these poems, at times under different titles or as separate poems, have appeared in *Southern Review*, *Third Coast*, *POOL*, *Southern Poetry Review*, *Spillway*, *Dogwood*, the *Texas Observer*, *RE:AL The Journal of Arts and Letters*, *farfelu*, *Concho River Review*, *San Antonio Express-News*, and the *Austin Chronicle*.

This book would not have been possible without the advice and editing of poet Nick Courtright. It was his suggestion to build from one poem an entire book in the voice of a fictional secretary to Wallace Stevens.

Kath Anderson, Bob Ayres, Alice Batt, Carole Buckman, Marcy Buffington, Gary Cooke, Ken Fontenot, Lynn Gilbert, Judith Infante, Monty Jones, and Andre Jordan made suggestions on these poems or kept me writing. Or both. Ellen and Joe Bell, Molly Bennett, Sharon Flournoy, Anne Freeman, Joan Hilgers, Jan King, Cynthia Levinson, Cristina Speligene, Sarah Stromeyer, and the Schenkkan and Victory families encouraged me over and over.

Our family has sustained me during this project. Thank you, Ben and Morena, Nate and Scout, and Zack and Camille. My husband Pete was with me when I learned this book would be published. That is exactly how I would have wished it.

CONTENTS

Ideas of Order

Harmonium

. . . she feels the dark / Encroachment
of that old catastrophe

Mr. and Mrs.

She could be Mrs. Baldwin.
She could be Mrs. Flynn.
All we know is, she's his secretary
and he is Mr. Stevens.

Today he is thanking Mr. van Geyzel
for the package from Ceylon. Mrs. Stevens
and Holly like the necklaces. Mr. Stevens
has put the Buddha in his room.

First lesson a secretary learns,
don't snoop. Take letters from dictation,
figure out the scraps of writing he brings in,
his poems, and always keep a carbon.

He's got a temper. Broke his hand,
she heard, in a brawl
with Hemingway in Key West.
She's used to a man's temper.

She's got a family to help support
in this godforsaken city.
Not a watermelon here worth spit.
She does love the first snow.

Before Mr. Stevens

For none of the others has she turned a scrawled *its*
into *it's* almost daily. None brought in roses,
cream, deep pink, wrapped in damp newspaper.
From Mrs. Stevens, he said, for my desk.

Her first boss was an uncle, Southern Plumbing
which expanded too fast. Next, her pastor
until he was called by a Texas congregation.
She'd had enough of church work anyway.

One boss wanted to give her a ride home.
When he offered the next night, too,
she began looking through the classifieds.
Mr. Stevens doesn't own a car, doesn't even drive.

Mr. Rubenstein had been kindest. No looking
over her shoulder or rifling through her desk
when she was at lunch. He was lucky
to have a college graduate, he said more than once.

She kept the lace gloves he gave her at Christmas
in tissue. By February he was dead.
With Mr. Stevens it was a surprisingly large check
and a card, *It's the Holidays!*, with *It's* underlined.

Wasps

Outside her son's bedroom, in a fist-sized nest,
yellow and black wasps doze on papery cells.
She thwacks the windowpane,
appalled that danger has come so close,
though her son is gone now, to college.

On their honeymoon, her husband surprised
a hive as they trudged home from a Greek beach.
The bees stung his face, his nose, inside his ears.
In panic, he knocked off his glasses
and had to go back into the swarm

while she begged the bees, "Oh! Stop! Stop!"
Later, in their whitewashed hotel by the sea,
they fell asleep to shouts and banged pots,
the drone of family life, which wasps know
all too briefly and for that she must apologize.

She, who admires fertility in any form,
curses their misfortune to have nested here.
No one thing will bring us to safety
or her firstborn back home, she knows that.
She will kill the wasps anyway.

She Encounters a Subtle Threat
from the Future

On the elevator, It's snowing,
she said almost to herself, and
It's good to be inside.

It's best from the cafeteria,
a man beside her said,
so she went up there on her break.

You were right, she told him later
passing in the hall. You see, you see,
he said, and that was enough—

that and how she had bowed her head
slightly, warming to his approval—
to warn her: steer clear.

A Silence So Huge, There Is No "I"

If friends ask her about Mr. Stevens at all,
they ask about the snow man poem,
what it means. I'm only the secretary,
she says, but the way the poem begins—
One must have the mind of winter—
fits Mr. Stevens to a T. No "I" for him.

As in his poem, the junipers and spruces
are all crusted with snow and ice today.
She steps outside to behold the nothing.
It might help her quiet down, as Mother
used to say. But quiet can get to her.
She'll be back at her typewriter soon.

Mr. Stevens' Hat Band

Some days not even one good look at the maples
dropping brilliant leaves or a glimpse but
only to remember ball moss on trees back home.

Thus, only this morning had she realized
that a black band was now on Mr. Stevens' felt hat.
When did it take the place of the brown one?

Was there a death? His brother Garrett?
She mailed a check to him the first of each month.
Mr. Stevens had said nothing. He wouldn't

and no use re-reading the lines of poetry
he gave her to type. The few details—
two pears, a bowl of carnations—tell her little.

It's our nature to be curious,
her psychiatrist said. But people
often keep parts of themselves separate,

in compartments. She thought of drawers
in one of her gunmetal gray filing cabinets.
One entire cabinet was labeled Father.

Her Father Sums Up

1.

They all graduated from college.
All nine graduated and on time.
I paid for my wife to go, too.

2.

I drove to Pineville to see Edward in the asylum.
I drove to the farm to visit my grandmother.
Bring Mary Grace, she wrote, *that precious child*.
And, *Here's a dollar. Bring sugar and stamps*.

3.

I bought good shoes and good suits
and good polish for my leather shoes.
I taught the girls to polish them.

4.

Lithium finally, and still I couldn't sleep.
Why shouldn't I talk all night?
The children needed to be told
that Cousin Gertie cheated me.
It wasn't every night. It wasn't always all night.

5.

I cried reading "The Charge of the Light Brigade,"
I cried at the site of the battle at Mansfield.
I cried singing at my second cousin's funeral
in Benton, Sunday afternoons at Sister Marie's,
driving home from the asylum, and I cried
at the very mention of my mother.
I cried reading the children *Out to Aunt Mary's.*

6.

Their mother wasn't ambitious.
She was smart enough.
She sewed for the girls and got everyone to school
on time and clean. She didn't complain.
She stayed with it and with me,
what choice did she have? Nine children.

Saturday Morning Gamble

At the hospital to see her friend,
she wends through the grim garage
past parking space after parking space

Reserved for Doctors
Brinkman, McCallum, Masterson, and Case.

It's Saturday, no one here to hear her complaint
about privilege and perks held tight
for absent doctors. The injustice, and July, smolder.

Then one doc's spot, saved for one Greenway alone—
weekends, New Year's—calls to her like home.

Her father once took himself to a hospital.
He couldn't sleep. He got electroshock,
the treatment then, a risk,

like parking where you should not.
To see him, her mother caught the trolley at Line,

her coat March-buttoned, lips tight, no tears.
She was forty-nine, a grown-up,
still hopeful about God, but ashamed,

weren't they all, and it's too much
to bear past red after red after red

You Will Be Towed From This Spot.
It's a risk, Dr. Greenway,
like letting go of God as a child of ten.

Asylum

Had Uncle Edward known
when he strolled away from the asylum
that the hundred miles back home to the farm

would be his last long freedom,
he might have stopped for pie in Pleasant Hill
or hitchhiked part of the way.

After he got home,
things were okay until again threats,
murderous threats she was told,

and they took Edward back to Pineville
where he stayed put fifty years
except for walks on the grounds.

～

As a child, she imagined a rescue—
dogs, barbed wire, Edward hurried
to the back seat of the old Chrysler,

her father swinging up the drive,
the mysterious uncle in frayed flannel
settling into the middle bedroom.

In fact, her father, close himself to breaking,
fought like mad when the state
threatened to release his only brother.

～

She was ashamed of him,
and scared: would he rescue her?
But had she known that sacrifice,

like freedom, has its limits,
and what we do for our children
we may not do for others,

she might have thought before now
of loss, and a man's grief,
as he Sunday-drove a hundred miles south.

Her Husband's Worth

A board member got her the job with Mr. Stevens,
that's how much the museum wanted her husband.

Another arranged a loan on a house. Donors
were then invited to *Meet The New Curator!*

She was asked about the children.
She asked about *their* children.

A descendant of Samuel Colt came
and people from Aetna and Travelers

and Hartford, too, but not Mr. Stevens
so she felt free to have a second cocktail.

She wore what she called her arty dress
(the one that led him to kiss her neck).

A board member back home once whispered
to be heard, That neckline is beyond shocking,

a comment the curator and his wife still mention
when they need another reason for why they left.

First Spring in Hartford, 1937

She hasn't found a church, hasn't tried.
She's not Baptist anymore. She's *something*.
She still prays, of course.

It's on her mind walking in Elizabeth Park.
Hartford Seminary is nearby;
she's seen a sign from the bus.

She walks in that direction.
There's a chain across the entrance—
Saturday—but a list of lectures is posted.

Halfway down, *The History of Islam.*
She knows nothing. She couldn't find crocuses
in the park, though a neighbor said they're out.

This is her time, isn't it?
She can just listen. She can sit in the back.
Like on the bus at home, she thinks, the Negroes.

Call and Response

What if she never looked for a church?
If she didn't go to church at all?
Even asking upset her. Sunday *was* church,
two services. But if here, new city,

new job, the day were entirely her own?
The *Hartford Courant* front to back
and later, she'd take herself to the park.

She tried, for months. Then, in defeat,
went to 11 o'clock at the seminary.
Next week, a Unitarian service. And
one Sunday slipped into Trinity

where she: sat in the back and eyed the door,
resolutely refused to bow to the cross,
stood when all around her knelt,

and snapped the prayer book closed
at *We are not worthy so much as to gather up
the crumbs under thy Table.* She'd had enough
of that where she came from. They were Baptists,

deep in sin. Regardless, *Hallelujah, Hallelujah,*
they sang, and, no poets,
they named the cat Sunshine.

Grocery Store Parking Lot Reverie

She stops. She has time. No one's with her,
what luck. No one is here to name this bird,
black rings on pale neck, a bald Picasso
in his famous striped tee.

The bird quick, quick walks across the pavement.
It's—*no*—this sorting of male and female, cardinal/
grackle must end. Eyes and ears only.
A minute passes. Good, good. Another

to her left, a second bird, smudged red throat quivering.
It's enough to be so close—*no*. Sing. The bird flies off.
Still, that red. She wills herself only to look.
It is not too late to receive this world.

The Man with the Blue Guitar

That I may reduce the monster to / Myself

Mr. Stevens Inquires
about Her Poetic Interests

Mr. Stevens this morning at her desk,
Do you read poetry? Edna St. Vincent Millay?
She has been given *The Ballad of the Harp-Weaver*
by her aunt, To keep you company up there.

I drank at every vine.
    The last was like the first.
I came upon no wine
    So wonderful as thirst.

Why didn't he say Marianne Moore?
She types his letters to her.
They seem to be great pals.
She has tried to read Miss Moore,

so clever. Millay is all passion.
Her own poems are nothing like theirs.
Not that she'd mention it.
Not that he'd ask.

Elegy for Her Father-in-Law

Everyone she's reading is grieving, too.
A woman carries her rocking chair
to the middle of a field. Another walks
the Galilee, camping in creek beds.
They will not be at home.

She is making biscuits.
If it takes all summer,
a biscuit that will not fail.
And if her husband pleads *Stop Stop*,
he can leave.

Biscuits, novels are not his way.
There are heron to quiet for,
all those trout. Let him come back:
she is unmoored in rooms unmanned.
A floury hell this kitchen, she says,

let's rend our clothes, everything off.
At last they are fully undone.
Soon the rocking can stop,
the tilted field steady itself:
the day is coming to an end.

Go home, woman walking the land.
Everyone dies. What a mess,
and all these biscuits, trout.
They ought to dress to eat.
That is what most people do.

Upon Virginia Woolf's Death, 1941

The close quarters of marriage,
of mouths to milky breast—
she thinks room after room
will open once she rooms alone.

Not a corner off the kitchen
but a bit of square beneath the stairs.
Her desk, husbanded—true—
and Monet hangs well on this blue

but the boys she bore? Borne away.
Her time for brooding has run.
Cleave to one art? To you?
The distant Thames is no mate.

Mother, do not hover so,
Holy, Holy, Holy humming.
It is deathly still here, in this room.
Virginia, *I thee*-Wait.

An Awakening

As a way of introducing herself,
she admires her neighbor's cap.
I'll knit you one, what color?

She doesn't want a cap.
She wants a friend
and takes over cookies.

Watching my weight,
the neighbor says,
and doesn't take the plate.

Good, her psychiatrist says,
and (as if to a child), You try it.
Say *No*. Are you able to do that?

This room smells. She notices
every week as she comes in.
Close to vanilla but sharper.

She tries it that night with her husband.
You saw the doctor, he sighs.
Let me know when you're better.

Mr. Stevens' Secretary Attempts a Fable

The cat worked her head into a milk bottle.
Father, Father, the children cried
and he took his hammer and tapped
until the bottle broke and curiosity could breathe.

A puzzle for the children:
how could Father be so loving to the cat
and shout so horribly at Mother?
They wished for her the same affection

as she hummed her hymns and slunk away.
She pretended not to hear when the children
called for her to come out of the dark wood.
Then Father grew ill. Mysteriously,

Mother re-appeared. She spoon-fed him milky toast
and even climbed into his bed. How she could
mystified the children as they mewed about,
heads in glass bottles wherever they roamed.

Despite Her Sisters, She Keeps Up Hope

She was eight and remembers the whole thing.

She tells the story again and again.

Her sisters say, Forget it, it was only a cat

and a long time ago. She has cats

and shows them great affection. One's on her bed

right now, or on the couch. She talks to them

as if they are babies. What help is a cat

when you're sick? Some say she is sick.

Father's not here now. He can't rescue anything.

Mr. Stevens' Secretary Considers
Point of View

Buzzing near her. A fat bee
is attacking nipple after brown nipple
of sunflower centers. She slant-cuts,

she rescues two for her desk.
Next day, pollen's gold blears the text—
accusing me, she writes. Why not

cheering me? She's angry at everything:
the sloping lawn off the parking lot,
the spruces and firs by the river

with their new growth. Spring, finally.
Her father planted daffodils next to the clothesline.
They came up brilliant year after yellow year.

Lady Bird

Bump then *Bump*, then silence. A bird has hit glass
out her window. What would be wrong with keeping

Bird as Object, trained to be seen and sweet heard?
Prettily caged and clean,

her catch would be a reversal: noble
nature trapped by woman, for once, and kept as

Thing to sing and mirror her, gracious woman,
kind to the lesser—

wait. This bird is markedly dull, a female
unadorned, though spirited, now hopping

from rock to ground. Sparrow, her double, *ma soeur*—
fly from her, quickly.

Mr. Stevens and His Secretary Pause

In the middle of giving dictation, he stops
and opens his right-hand desk drawer.
He takes out a sheet of paper and adds
to what he's written. He'll be awhile with his poem.

She draws a stick figure on her steno pad.
It's a woman with curly hair, dancing.
Mr. Stevens goes dancing in NY with friends.
She draws a little table and adds cocktails.

The woman might order another,
young as the night is. She's a modern now,
she's not at home anymore, snapping beans
with her mother to *Goodnight, Irene*.

But this is fantasy. A secretary is not
a dancer, curly-haired and alive.
Maybe some secretaries, just not this one,
unsure of her feet, from the South, waiting.

She Begins Short Story after Short Story

The trampoline's his idea, something to get the kids outside.

Someone finally noticed her. Called her sweetie pie and left poems and flowers on the creaking childhood porch. Her father threatened to shoot him.

Please, a girl dream, a unicorn or a knight. Instead, the frame house as if for the shame of it and the apartment of brown towels. First Baptist when it was still downtown appears in warm golds.

He'd make her a swing and hang it from the front yard pecan and then she would notice the red oak before all its leaves dropped. Nothing much, a slatted back and seat, painted green like the earrings her sister got her. He'd make a pecan pie. She was fine, long as there was pie, she used to say, before these one-foot-in-front-of-the-other days.

The line must be perfectly straight, straight as the taut string my pencil follows but does not touch. The mind must not wander. Someone else's canvas edge-to-edge green, female hummingbirds fluttering to feed, but for me, lines and the light between, only light, broken and bound by graphite. Not for everyone this order. I came to it myself from elsewhere.

They listened for trouble, thunder, gunshot.

After Hours

Mr. Stevens, turning on a light, signed the papers
there in the hall. He was still in his suit and tie.
He thanked her for bringing them to the house
and past eight, but didn't ask after her.

Music was coming from another room. Bruckner,
he said, the Seventh Symphony.
He stepped toward the door. Time to leave.
She heard the light switched off behind her.

The rain had stopped. She stood by the car.
She didn't try to decide if she liked the music
but wondered if this is what he did most nights.
If so, she was glad for him.

She was glad and envious, of his knowledge,
of this gracious house. Why was it kept so dark?
Maybe to him that was restful.
She tried to imagine the dark being restful.

The Absence of Romance in Her History

A good day in a good city
that still does not call to her
in the evening dews and damps
like the one long left, and gladly.

She misses the piney woods.
Not the high-strung house,
time to dress again for church.

~

She cannot keep up with the trees.
Always a tree to name
as if to know: *honey locust.*

Today in the park she touched
triangular needles from China.
A couple was lying nearby on a quilt.

~

She is writing a memoir:
A poor swimmer, I gain land
mainly by floating the tides.
If I reach the island of three pines,
will I be content?

What Else?

A boy pushes a girl,
herself, on a swing at night in a park.

The boy loves her. She loves him:
he is like no one else, clever, funny,

his back beautiful, even as he walks away.
Alone now, the girl must slow the swing

and somehow stand. To look about her
at such a time did not occur to her.

There were pines. It was summer or late spring.
What else? The park was across from a school,

children played there at recess. What else?
Was it the park where he left her? her front porch?

Hartford Retreat

The asylum's grounds were designed
by the man who laid out Central Park.
She consoles herself with this.

Also, she is not her poor uncle:
just because she sees a psychiatrist
doesn't mean she will lose her mind.

Patients are free to walk the grounds
at *Hartford Retreat,* her doctor said.
A meadow leads to the Connecticut.

She'd like to go.
It's an urge no one need know about:
to walk between the line of trees,

a calm landscape for the insane.
A thanksgiving of sorts, for her doctor.
That she's getting help.

A Daughter Sums Up

She's told her psychiatrist about the cat
and the milk bottle. It's our nature
to be curious, he says. Why not enjoy it?

The image of the silky gold cat
licking its whiskers. The children
finding her, stuck, over and over.

What if Father had not rescued the cat?

That's a chance we take, the doctor says.
The bottle might have milk.
The cat is happy, if only for awhile.

She Takes a Letter
to Mr. Henry Church, 1942

Here's the church, here's the steeple,
(her fingers twitch to join together)
open the doors, see all the people:

Mr. Henry Church in French cuffs,
in her imagination, a pinstripe suit,
heir to the Arm & Hammer fortune

and the friend Mr. Stevens is writing.
Holly wants to drop out of Vassar,
he's been to Poughkeepsie *to no avail.*

He closes with greetings to Mrs. Church.
Is she a woman who comes and goes
from the Waldorf, as in Mr. Stevens' poem?

No, make her stunning, a model.
Mrs. Stevens could have been a model,
it's her profile on the Mercury dime.

She posed for their artist landlord
in New York, Mr. Stevens said.
They hadn't been married long.

How would he have courted?
My Dear Elsie in his fine hand and then
later, whispering it to her in the night.

She Writes a Version of Herself into Exodus

She made her way down the mountain.
Men hiding in the bushes grabbed at her
and one of the tablets broke. So the words

for her people this time were brief,
it couldn't be helped.
She kept to what was in stone.

They felt her face,
which later they would describe to the sick
and the lame as shining: *like oil.*

The people watched her begin, again,
to climb. She took no weapon.
Would God return? If the voice did not come,

she would—what? She could not stay
overnight; her mother would worry.
Her boyfriend had offered to come.

She passed where the thieves often were
and took off her veil, no need to hide now.
She began to cry.

And then: *You.*
Not unkindly.
Give me your hand.

She's Hoping It Wasn't God

who killed that baby,
the one the Bible doesn't name, begat
when the king lay with Bathsheba,
all clean from her periodic bathing,
her cuckolded husband soon sent to die a hero.

It hardly seems just:
the adulterers screw up, the innocents pay.
What a state the king got into, fasting
and praying for the little one's life.
When it didn't work, he lightened up:

would weeping bring Baby Blank back?
On with the lovemaking!

Solomon, the newlyweds named the next one:
"peace." God called him Jedidiah,
"beloved of the Lord." Two tags for that boy,
that's nice, and surely the other kid
then got a name. Something fine, like David.

When She Tired of the Bible

At lunch, as she ate each red grape,
feeling its slight roughness on her tongue,
she read from *The Man with the Blue Guitar.*

She liked seeing the words she first typed
and found herself marking lines here and there
as if she might get back to the poems later.

    Nothing must stand

Between you and the shapes you take
When the crust of shape has been destroyed.

But it was "The Yellow Wall-paper"
she was reading at home—though she shouldn't.
Charlotte Perkins Gilman killed herself.

She feels she is past danger of that sort.
She's never said anything to Mr. Stevens.
Just a day off here and there.

Ideas of Order

Re-statement of Romance

Mr. Stevens' Voice

It's one way at nine a.m., another after lunch
when he returns from the Canoe Club and,
she's heard, martinis. She imagines
his view of the sparkling Connecticut
bordered by fir trees still new to her.

After lunch, almost a giggle.
A bit of showing off, too.
Young Mr. Ardway might be sent
to the library if he doesn't know
the meaning of a word: *ellipse*.

He doesn't send her, but he might tease
again about her accent. Early on
she had pronounced the word *iron*
EYE-ron, like back home.
She hasn't made that mistake again.

Her father read Tennyson,
Half a league, half a league, / Half a league onward,
All in the valley of Death / Rode the six hundred
in a big voice, his arms sweeping,
that signaled to the children possible tears.

She's heard that in Mr. Stevens' voice.
One time, when he was on the phone to Holly

or perhaps it was Mrs. Stevens
he was talking to, a woman anyway.
A woman could bring him close to tears.

You'd never know that from mornings
spent dictating letters as head of surety,
Hartford Accident and Indemnity.
That voice, the tearful one, drew her in,
and she wished it did not.

Mr. Stevens Will Pass

He has been invited to contribute
to a symposium on Ezra Pound
and what he said on the radio.

Mr. Stevens says he can see both sides of it—
that Pound is traitorous, that he is not.
Still, he wants to stay out of it.

And his letter is not to be quoted,
that's how he put it, *or used in any way*.
But, if Pound comes to America and wants help

and *shows he is entitled to it,* ok,
Mr. Stevens will help. A lot of *ifs*,
she thinks.

Fidelity

Oriental, she decides of his smell,
but that may be because of the tea.
Picked this up in Hong Kong,
his friend wrote in a casual hand.
White peony tea. Mr. Stevens was pleased.

His smell is earthier than a flower,
she told her psychiatrist. Is it okay to notice?
He said, Can you help noticing?

She could have said
    I'm his secretary
    I'm married
    I'm a mother.

Instead she now sometimes dabs
Chantilly behind each ear.
Why not? her doctor would say.
No need to tell him the pretty bottle
is kept not at home but in her desk.

Marriage, Another Year

He brings flowers from the wild
as if she might yet throw over tulips.

    [Cezanne's wife is falling left.
    He has always painted her; lately, at a tilt.]

At times the flowers are not wild
but he never brings tulips now.

    [Matisse's woman in bronze
    by the fourth relief is mere suggestion.]

What if not tulips is his understanding?

She means, of me.
She means, of late.

    ~

His body insists
resists.
Her body could
should.

Insists, resists, she writes.
She'll leave in both. Could and should.

    [Like the quick pencil Picasso kept
    left in *The Charnel House*.

Matisse, too, sometimes didn't erase
his starts, the failures.]

This *his her*
has been going on for some time.
A work, viewed generously,
of some force.

～

He was alone in the field
when cranes lifted from the high grass.

Eight birds pull east,
the plain behind them treeless.

They framed the photo
he took for over the bed.

She saw the cranes, too,
blur of white and black, stick legs,

she was there beside him.
He forgets until he is above her.

～

She insisted: red dressers
for either side of the window.

They had to be red.

The neighbor's second story
so close, they close the shutter.

On the red, yellow tulips.
The jumbles of field flowers

he brings home don't last,
she keeps telling him,

so he brings more.

～

Deceit is inimical to light
beneath the stained glass.

She could on a day like today,
leaves falling, rain coming, be glass.

Not Mary, blue-weeping at the cross.
Clear.

[Now there's something new—
isn't bloody, staining red more you?]

Any light today would be beheld.
And night could be seen through.

~

Bee-buzzing plum tree
she didn't choose you, he did.

His white blossoms,
his the gray-ringed trunk.

Birds are his. If she were bird,
would that she please.

[The widow O'Keeffe hated
how her flowers became to some

a woman's sex, and her undulating
purple mountains, a woman
lying on her side.]

Piano's hers, just hymns,
hardly the Beethoven

now drawing him in.
Down the street children

call to each other. Days
dim pink to coral to less.

~

Who wants anymore
to read about love

women in love
then out of love

single girl single girl
walking the poor park

saved by cherry blossoms
spring after spring

who wants anymore
to read about spring.

Wonder Woman

She's in the corner drugstore
with another headache from hell
when in walks who but Mrs. Stevens

just as her son waves a comic: Wonder Woman
in a red bustier embroidered with an eagle,
blue underpants, and high-heeled boots.

For a moment, they are a tableau—
Woman Frowning, Young Man with Comic,
Fur-Coated Matron Gliding Past.

I'll take it on the train.
Something to show the other recruits.
God knows, she's no Wonder Woman

in thought, word or deed. If she were,
the bad guys would be on the run
and her youngest not called up to Camp Lee.

She will be taking some time off.
Family, she has told Mr. Stevens.
True enough, for now.

Pied a Terre

Now, the sound of trombones—yes—
and drums. She climbs onto the fire escape
of the apartment she's rented for a month

and sees three floors below a procession
of reds and golds. There's a float
and on it a statue and dark-suited men.

An acolyte swings incense; children
are singing. At Our Lady of Pompeii
on the corner the worshippers stop

and go in. She would have waved.
Next, a fly rubs its front legs together,
nods its orange head, then is gone.

This is it: a fly and a parade of sorts.
No one is coming for lunch or dinner.
The feather she found just off Sixth Avenue

weighs nothing, so she brought it home.
The seagull didn't lose it for her.
She wouldn't ask it to.

O Savage Spirit

Please, a girl dream, a unicorn or a knight.
Instead the Father-built house as if for the shame of it.

Awake, the usual relief.
From the apartment window, she sees a robin
land on a chimney, newly bricked. Money.

The gulls stay close to the river
many here claim a view of.

In her dream, she re-builds a pyramid of backyard figs.
The teenage bully next door skulks by.
She guards the figs, though she's no longer of that place.

〜

It is the habit of mourning doves to while away
precious time on fire escapes, and her habit

for now is to be grateful if even one lands
on the rusted railing she does not trust for herself.
She loved this morning's earliest dove,

how content it seemed, how little it pecked at itself.
That was a dove she could live beside.

〜

In the dream, she re-arranged the downstairs.
They'll sleep in the dining room. No, wrong house.

She is frightening herself. She doesn't tell anyone.
There's God for night terrors and God, or what's right,
reminds her not to frighten even birds.

She can stand slowly. She can approach windows quietly.
A rusty ladder leads to the building's roof.

She dreams of climbing, up up.
Birds are flying away, playing it safe.
They'll come back, they know she's not reliably here.

Dead Cloud Season

Everywhere fewer mourning doves
than white wings, but why it matters

she forgets or why today the air lacks currents
and so it's said, it is dead cloud season,

a good term for her in this rented kitchen
with a bad landscape of mountains, a lake

and a man steadying his oars,
not moving away with certainty

or toward peaks so painterly
they almost endear the earnest centering

of boat and man alone,
except for trees turning to red

so it must be fall, it must be
despite the majesty these mountains imply

the true subject is steadiness
under clouds so hopeless they are lost.

The News from Hartford

The children refused.
They were Negro girls, some only 13,
and they refused.

   Inside, they insisted,
they were told they'd work inside.
They'd been hired from the street

for a shade tobacco farm.
A photo of the tents ran above the story.
Who knew tobacco was grown indoors?

They must have been desperately poor.
Only a generation since her own family—
her husband's, too—grew cotton,

though that was different: they grew it,
not picked it. And now these girls,
July, wanting to be out of the heat.

Instead, they walked home eleven miles.
Their parents called the Mayor.
This is Hartford, not the South,

she thinks, and reads the story again.
These are not her people.
But about that, how should she feel?

Of Mere Being

Her list of attainments

(*I got up the mountain*
—or most of the way)

was in the making
when the bird flashed red
with glistening black wings.

Her list of failures, too

(*I didn't reach the great monastery,*
not even the prayer flags).

Alone, coming off the mountain,
she stills herself,
hoping to more fully receive

and if not (*How quickly*
I consider failure),

to let it be.

The Good Husband

He failed at first to get the bedroom ceiling fixture to take its light bulb and then went back at it the next morning and, deciding he'd better take the whole housing down, he gently inserted the bulb again and screwed it in until it couldn't take it anymore.

Light!

Your hero, he left in a note.

Her first thought is to flee the house. He expects something in return. A kiss. He wants more. He knows not to ask. It could be simple: light is restored. Not so easy for them.

Marriage Therapy

Digging again to China with no thought
until now of waterlines and waste
they might strike shoveling up
backyard grass for a garden.

How childlike, to trust
this dark earth holds nothing
they should leave alone.

The ground they dig, sweating, tight-lipped
brings forth concrete chunks from an old drive.
Some call whatever they find finds.
But they were born in the year of the pig:

two pigs create their own trouble.
It's not the digging—that's natural enough.
It's believing a garden will come of it.

A Higher Form

These lurches

in the evolution of

the long-paired

could mean a higher form
is in the making.

Not for them

the eons it might take
to alter barbs to nubs

then gone.

They've had to seize the moment
(reproducing as they were).

If fittest means less friction,

if nature's surest bet turns out
to be two,

they'll survive,

a theory they'll keep
testing.

Back to Work

It's far more than she wants to know. But she's his secretary
and someone has to type the letters to the lawyers.
His daughter is divorcing. It's already taken two years.

Far more than she *should* know. But she isn't going to tell
anyone. Mr. Stevens dictates with his head down.
He keeps swiveling his chair away from her.

Far be it for her to judge. Hasn't she just been
thinking through her own marriage?
The letters she's typing confirm it: no thanks.

Having a grandson seems to cheer Mr. Stevens.
It's his job, and sometimes hers, too, to run after him
when Holly's signing papers to get this thing over with.

Mr. Stevens and His Secretary, Five Years Later

The Knopfs' kind words on the Pulitzer
have been acknowledged,
she did that this morning.

If necessary, she will compose the letters
herself; she already signs for him.
She will check her spelling, her old burden,

she tells him. He manages a smile.
They have always tried
to be courteous to each other.

She has brought a mustard-colored bowl
from home. She did not have white.
Carnations are too dear, dahlias will do.

To his nurses, he quotes Longfellow:
Listen, my children, and you shall hear . . .
In her South, it was *Evangeline*,

a romance with a beginning and an end.
Mr. Stevens didn't write romances.
A world of clear water, brilliant-edged . . .

At His Service, 1955

Why in sex is it called "coming?"
In the novel she's reading, "the rush."
She can't believe she's thinking about this.

A year ago, Mr. Stevens was practicing
in his office to record poems for Harvard,
pausing slightly after each phrase as if
he were a commencement speaker.

Are you The Coming One?
John sent his disciples to ask Jesus.
I'm alive, as she stands to sing. *I'm alive.*

Mr. Stevens' Secretary
Transcribes a Poem

"Green?" Mr. Stevens might have written "green."
He had just come back from Florida.
Was "green," if it *was* "green,"
his way to say "fresh?" No help from him.
If she typed "green" and he meant "grown,"
on handing the sheet back, Mr. Stevens
would only marvel again at her words per minute.
There were snaps of his daughter under palms
and he passed out saltwater taffy.
Atlantic City's was better.
If only he'd dictate.
In shorthand, she would begin "green"
as a little hill sloping into a valley.
The line would turn up again, curl into a loop
and end level as if out on the plain. Mr. Stevens,
walking through snow, scribbling, wouldn't be thinking
of the hill any secretary knew was "g."
He'd re-fold his piece of paper. The office was ahead.
She'd be at her desk.

NOTES

The title of the poem "The Absence of Romance in Her History" comes from Thucydides' *The History of the Peloponnesian War*:

> The absence of romance in my history will, I fear, detract somewhat from its interest; but I shall be content if it is judged useful by those inquirers who desire an exact knowledge of the past as an aid to the interpretation of the future.

I have used biographical information for these poems from a number of sources, including

> *Wallace Stevens: Collected Poetry and Prose*, ed. Frank Kermode and Joan Richardson (New York: Library of America, 1997), esp. the Letters section and the Chronology which follows.

> *The Collected Letters of Wallace Stevens*, selected and ed. by Holly Stevens (Berkeley: University of California Press, 1966).